AF615228

The Kiss of Peace

by

Colin Buchanan

Principal, St. John's College, Bramcote, Nottingham

Member of the Church of England Liturgical Commission

GROVE BOOKS

BRAMCOTE NOTTS.

CONTENTS

Copyright Colin Buchanan 1982

THE COVER PICTURE

is by Peter Ashton

PREFACE

I think this is the longest treatment ever published on this subject! Even so I was conscious of a need to stop it going on growing as I wrote it. I was also very conscious that it is currently not fully settled down, and that minds are still changing about it. I checked out how my own had moved over the years, and discovered the following:

(i) 'It has been restored . . . in the Church of South India. Englishmen are Englishmen, no doubt, and so no handclasp is prescribed in this text. However it is most certainly the point at which we ought to recall that we belong to each other in Jesus Christ . . .' (December 1966, re Series 2, in *A Guide to the New Communion Service* (Church Book Room Press)).

(ii) 'Handclasps are a problem to Englishmen. But difficulties ought not to prevent a congregation striving at a goal.' (October 1972, re the Parish Communion (on the eve of authorization of Series 3) in *Patterns of Sunday Worship* (Grove Booklet on Ministry and Worship no. 9, first edition).

(iii) 'I note . . . on re-reading the first edition how cautious I then was about the Kiss of Peace . . .' (October 1975, in the Introduction to the second edition of *Patterns of Sunday Worship*).

(iv) 'The Kiss of Peace in communion exemplifies the freedom [to use our bodies] very well . . . This is by no means exclusive to charismatics . . .' (May 1977, in *Encountering Charismatic Worship* (Grove Booklet on Ministry and Worship no. 51)).

(v) 'The words . . . are about peace between believers *because they are in Christ.* The actions should show it. And when believers grasp each other by the hand, or embrace, then their words to each other should be warm. The people of God are now ready to feast together.' (November 1980, in *Anglican Worship Today* (Collins, 1980)).

That is a reminder to me at least that this cannot be a final and definitive treatment. I can only add that in this booklet if in no other, when it comes to personal pronouns the male embraces the female.

C.O.B.

First Impression April 1982

ISSN 0144–1728

ISBN 0 907536 21 2

1. THE BIBLICAL KISS

The Bible has a good share of embracing and kissing. These are not usually erotic in character, though occasionally they may be (as, e.g., in Song of Solomon 1.2 and—perhaps with ambivalent meaning—in 8.1). More regularly the significance is of reconciliation after enmity (as, e.g., in Genesis 33.4) or after a long parting (as e.g., in Genesis 45.15). There is also considerable precedent in the Old Testament for the kiss used at parting (cf. Gen. 50.1, which actually follows death, Ruth 1.10 (and its companion verse Ruth 1.14), 1 Sam. 20.41 and 2 Sam. 19.39). None of the texts cited is particularly 'liturgical', though in Genesis 50 the act is slightly more ritualistic than when given to a living person who can appreciate it, and in 1 Samuel 20.41 the act is followed by a semi-ritual 'dismissal'.[1] These are kisses shared between persons of the same sex as each other, and very clearly non-erotic. The physical embrace, with presumably the touching of cheeks if not of lips, is undertaken quite naturally and gives special significance to a relationship[2]. It is paralleled today when Middle Eastern and even Iron Curtain country leaders descend from jet aircraft and embrace each other on either cheek, in a way which we rarely see Mrs. Thatcher or President Reagan using. Eastern Orthodox prelates use similar greetings with church leaders, but most Westerners seem to have difficulty in getting back into this Ancient Eastern world.

The New Testament reflects the same atmosphere. When Jesus goes to the home of the Pharisee (Luke 7.36-50) and is anointed by the prostitute, part of Jesus' rebuke to his host is 'you gave me no kiss' (7.45). Presumably a guest was likely to expect a kiss from his host, and the Pharisee had deliberately snubbed him. It might well be unusual—even scandalous—for a street-woman to give a man a kiss as then happened, though the form and manner of her kissing of Jesus' feet was clearly not erotic. There are perhaps some hints of the meaning of the kiss amongst Christians of a later generation in the association with her kiss of both the forgiveness of sins and the mention of peace (7.47, 50). The corollary of the kiss which the Pharisee ought to have given is the kiss which Judas ought not to have attempted (Luke 22.47-48). The offence of the kiss here—a kiss which should have meant loyalty and peace—is exactly the same as the offence of breaking bread with someone and then betraying him ('the hand of him who is going to betray me is with mine on the table', Luke 22.21). Presumably both breaking bread and giving a kiss establish a bond which is supposed to be unbreakable. The events of the night of the Last Supper are the background to the Christian eucharistic celebration. The offence of Judas etches by contrast the true Christian theme of love—for the feast is a feast of love (indeed an 'agape'), and the kiss is a kiss of love.[3]

[1] In the light of later liturgical language, it is intriguing to note the accompanying 'Go in *peace*' in this passage. The dismissal in 2 Samuel 19.39 also has a 'semi-liturgical' character to it.

[2] There is also a notion of appeasing or propitiating a master or lord—cf. Ps. 2.12. Is this the origin of kissing bishops' rings . . . ? (But the ASB Psalter suppresses 'kiss' here!)

[3] 'Kiss of love' is actually used as the description in 1 Peter 5.16.

It is only a small step from the love which characterized the infant church to the title of their corporate meal as a 'love-feast'[1], and to the practice of exchanging a 'holy kiss' (Rom. 16.16, 1 Cor. 16.20, 2 Cor. 13.12, 1 Thess. 5.26, cf. 1 Pet. 5.14). From the standpoint of later liturgical history these references to the 'kiss' are infuriatingly reticent at two significant points, but the general practice is easily demonstrable from these instructions by both Paul and Peter. The two points at which we would have liked a morsel more information are as follows:

1. The five references do not locate the kiss as beyond dispute within a liturgical context. The case that this is a *liturgical* kiss cannot be proven. On the other hand, it is difficult to *prove* a liturgical context for anything very much in the New Testament—and the reason is that the New Testament church was not ready to define a 'liturgical context' in the way later church life has had to do.[2] When the people of God 'came together' (1 Cor. 11.20, cf. 14.26) they did whatever they had to do, and apparently made little distinction between what we would call a 'service' (with a distinct liturgical beginning and ending) and what we would call 'business' (and handle in a different way).[3] It is clear that the 'kiss' was part of what they were to do when they had assembled at least to hear the particular apostolic letter read out, and presumably to do whatever else had to be done. So the event might qualify as 'worship', granted the differences between them and us.

   It would be rather harder to insist that it must have been eucharistic worship. There are hints of 'liturgy' in the various contexts—and the use of the word 'holy' to qualify 'kiss' suggests that it is a churchly context in which the kiss is given.[4] In 1 Corinthians 16 there is a greeting from a church in a house in Asia (16.19). Was the letter going to a similar gathering? Certainly the collection (16.1-4) has a churchly look to it, and the Marana Tha (16.22) is a kind of liturgical exclamation. The other passages similarly show that the letters are expected to be read in a main assembly of the local church (see 1 Thess. 5.13-28 in particular), and that is the nearest to a 'liturgical' context that we can ask. It would look from these contexts as though the second century and later practice developed by linear descent from these beginnings.

[1] 'Agape' is used meaning a 'love-feast' love-feast' in Jude 12, and in post-apostolic authors (e.g. Ignatius *Smyrneans* 8). For a fuller discussion of the agape see Trevor Lloyd *Agapes and Informal Eucharists* (Grove Booklet on Ministry and Worship no. 19, 1973—currently out of print).

[2] Thus the incident in Acts 20.36-37 (where there was both prayer and kissing!) is not amenable to the question, was this liturgical?

[3] See my discussion of this point in my *Leading Worship* (Grove Worship Series no. 76, 1981) p.7.

[4] I suppose a wholly innocent English reader *could* imagine that 'holy' here meant 'chaste' (which the holy kiss must certainly be!), but the general use of *hagios* ('holy') suggests that it is a word used to mark off the 'saints' (or 'holy ones') from the world.

2. The other lacuna from the standpoint of later liturgical history is that the kiss is nowhere described as the 'kiss of peace', let alone as the 'peace' on its own. It is the kiss of greeting[1], and certainly the kiss of love. 'Peace' is quite closely juxtaposed to the kiss in three of the five contexts (see 2 Cor. 13.11, 1 Thess. 5.23, and 1 Pet. 5.14).[2] But the most characteristic description of the kiss is that it is 'holy', and the later addition of the word 'peace' cannot be clearly traced to the New Testament.

   That is not to ignore the implications of the word 'peace' in the New Testament. Because in the later authors the kiss so quickly became the 'kiss of peace'[3], it is clear that the biblical understanding of 'peace' would be important to an exhaustive treatment. *Shalom* and the Greek equivalent *eirene* are used both as greetings and as concepts of profound force.[4]

What is wholly clear to us from above discussion, along with our other knowledge of the eucharist and the church in the New Testament, is that the church was intensely concerned for its internal 'social' relationships. Unity and love were no mere extras to church life—they were integral to being the church at all. The kiss expressed and conserved this dimension.

[1] Whilst the actual words 'kiss of greeting' does not occur, yet the *aspasmos/aspazomai* ('greeting'/'greet') words are found inextricably bound together with the kiss (three times in Rom. 16.16, five times in 1 Cor. 16.19-21, twice in 2 Cor. 13.12, once in 1 Thess 5.26, twice in 1 Pet. 5.13-14).

[2] And in Rom. 16.16-17 there is a warning against division.

[3] See page 7 below.

[4] See, for example, Matt. 10.13, John 14.27, John 20.21, Phil. 4.7, Heb. 13.20, and the opening and closing of epistles. Some of the force of these is found in 'Go in peace . . .'.

2. THE KISS IN THE EARLY LITURGIES

The first and most famous reference to the kiss in the early literature is to be found in Justin Martyr's account of the baptismal liturgy:

> 'After we have thus baptized him who has believed . . . we take him to those who are called brethren where they are assembled to make common prayers earnestly for ourselves and for him who has been enlightened and for all others everywhere . . . When we have ended the prayers, we greet one another with a kiss. Then bread and a cup of water and of mixed wine are brought . . .'[1]

The following paragraphs in Justin go on with a second account of the eucharist, this time of the weekly Sunday celebration, but in this account the kiss is not mentioned, though it must surely have occurred? The next straight account with which we are concerned comes in the *Apostolic Tradition* of Hippolytus, and again concerns a baptismal eucharist. This time there is a kind of 'two-stage' kiss:

> 'And having signed (the candidate) . . . he shall give him a kiss and say:
>
> "The Lord be with you."
>
> And he who has been signed shall say:
>
> "And with your spirit."
>
> So let him do with each one. And then they shall pray together with all the people: they do not pray with the faithful until they have carried out these things. And when they have prayed, they shall give the kiss of peace.'[2]

Thus the candidate for baptism is given a kiss by the bishop as the conclusion of the initiation ceremonies[3], but that kiss belongs with the initiatory liturgy, and is apparently distinguishable from the general exchange of the 'kiss of peace'; and when the neophytes have joined in

[1] Justin *Apology* 1.65 (translation in R. C. D. Jasper and G. J. Cuming (eds.) *Prayers of the Eucharist: Early and Reformed* (Collins, 1975) p.18).

[2] Hippolytus *Apostolic Tradition* ch. 21 (translation in G. J. Cuming (ed.) *Hippolytus: A Text for Students* (Grove Liturgical Study no. 8, 1976) pp.20.21).

[3] It should be noted that this 'two-stage' kiss seems to be the exception rather than the rule at baptism. Not all baptismal accounts make mention of the kiss at all (thus it does not appear in Tertullian's *De Baptismo* where we might have expected it), and those which do mention it tend to record only one kiss, more like that in Justin. Thus Chrysostom, to take but one later writer, says:

> 'As soon as they come up from those sacred waters all present embrace them, greet them, kiss them, congratulate and rejoice with them, because those who before were slaves and prisoners have all at once become free men and sons who are invited to the royal table. For as soon as they come up from the font, they are led to the awesome table which is laden with good things. They taste of the body and blood of the Lord . . .' (*Baptismal Homily* II, para 27, translation from E. J. Yarnold (ed.) *The Awe-Inspiring Rites of Initiation* (St. Paul Publications, 1972) p.169).

On the other hand there is one later development which suggests this specific bishop-to-candidate baptismal kiss—see page 13 below.

the prayers they are then for the first time able to *give* the kiss. It looks as though to be participant in the prayers was a new privilege which was part of the inclusion of the newcomer within the assembly, and thus qualified him for the giving of the kiss. It tallies exactly with Justin's order shown above.

Hippolytus also mentions the kiss in his description of the consecration of a bishop:

> 'When he has been made bishop, all shall offer the kiss of peace, greeting him because he has been made worthy. Then the deacons shall present the offering to him; and he, laying his hands on it with all the presbytery, shall give thanks, saying: . . .'[1]

This seems to be a combination of the two 'stages' noted above in the baptismal eucharist. It has both the element of welcome which properly follows the act of ordination, and also the air of being the general kiss which comes as part of the approach to the table and to the eucharistic action. Its place is unmistakably that which we find in Justin and in the other Hippolytan account.

The two Hippolytan accounts are of interest to us not only because they sustain Justin's position in the rite, but also because both of them use the title 'kiss of peace'. Here the two terms 'kiss' and 'peace' are found together in a strictly liturgical context for the first time. They belong together still today.

However, there is another intriguing reference to the 'kiss of peace' in a writer from a few years before the *Apostolic Tradition,* that is, in Tertullian as follows:

> 'Another custom has become prevalent. Such as are fasting withhold the kiss of peace, which is the seal of prayer, after prayer made with brethren. But when is peace more to be concluded with brethren than when, at the time of some religious observance, our prayer ascends with more acceptability; that they may themselves participate in our observance, and thereby be mollified for transacting with their brother touching their own peace? What prayer is complete if divorced from the "holy kiss?" Whom does peace impede when rendering service to his Lord? What kind of sacrifice is that from which men depart without peace? Whatever our prayer be, it will not be better than the observance of the precept by which we are bidden to conceal our fasts; for *now,* by abstinence from the kiss, we are known to be fasting. But even if there be some reason *for this practice,* still, lest you offend against this precept, you may perhaps defer your "peace" *at home*, where it is not possible for your fast to be entirely kept secret. But wherever else you can conceal your observance, you ought to remember the precept: thus you may satisfy the requirements of Discipline abroad and of custom at home. So, too, on the day of the passover, when the religious observance of a fast is general, and as it were public, we justly forego the kiss, caring nothing to conceal anything which we do in common with all.'[2]

[1] *op. cit.* ch. 4 (Cuming p.10).

[2] Tertullian *De Oratione* ch. 18 (translation in *The Ante-Nicene Fathers* (Eerdmans edition, Grand Rapids, 1957) Vol. III, p.686).

Here the title 'kiss of peace' is so taken for granted that the act can be called simply the 'peace'. However, the argument has caused a little confusion among scholars.[1] What does Tertullian mean by calling the kiss the 'seal of prayer'? Is he saying something about the kiss which would have a wider implication than its meaning at the eucharist? He certainly appears to be doing so. The argument seems to proceed on the basis that after two or more have joined together in prayer, they then usually joined each other in the 'kiss' to 'complete' the praying. This would make the kiss a kind of acted 'amen' to each other's prayers. Certainly a home context for such praying is envisaged just as much as a church context.

However, granted the discussion above about the relationship of the prayers of the faithful to the kiss in Justin and Hippolytus, it would be possible to contend that the kiss derived from a eucharistic context, obtained its meaning from that context, and was only used in a non-sacramental prayer context by derivation from that. At the eucharist the prayers did come just before the kiss.[2] Then the general meaning of the kiss which has been starting to emerge—that is, that it is part of the church's act of self-recognition at the eucharist—would not be imperilled by the Tertullian passage which links it only with prayers, but rather would be presupposed by it.

There may also be some passing interest in the understanding of the kiss which had led Christians *not* to share it. If they ceased from it when they were fasting, did they do so solely to advertise that they were fasting? Again, we have to say, surely not? There must have been a rationale which was at first blush plausible (and speciously humble?) in any explanations they gave. Was it then that they thought of the kiss as slightly too joyful an occurrence to go with fasting? Or was there still some close link in people's minds between the kiss and the love-feast, such to make the former inappropriate without the latter? Tertullian seems to be allowing some such point himself when he allows abstention from the kiss at passover, as then everyone is fasting. We are left with a vague impression of the kiss as an act with overtones of celebration and joy, which might be properly left aside when the whole church was fasting, though it was not to be omitted by any individual (lest he proclaim his fasting before men) when the rest of the church was practising it.

By now we are getting a growing impression that by the beginning of the third century the 'peace' had a strong atmosphere of 'peace between brethren' about it. And this in turn brings us to another strand of early church thought to which the kiss is later related, namely, the reconciliation of members of the church with each other. It is there

[1] Thus the Liturgical Commission in England could only draw attention to the Tertullian reference without reconciling it with the other evidence adduced here (*The Alternative Service Book 1980: A Commentary by the Liturgical Commission* (C.I.O., 1980) p.76, and note 30 on that page).

[2] See the quotation from Justin on page 6 above.

everywhere in the New Testament.[1] It gains a hold on the later centuries' minds in the text of Mattew 5.23-24:

> 'Therefore if you are offering your gift upon the altar, and there remember that your brother has something against you, then leave your gift there before the altar, and go off; first be reconciled to your brother, and then come and offer your gift.'

In days when the eucharist was expounded as the 'offering', then it was natural to connect this text with being reconciled before sharing in the eucharist—in other words, making 'peace'. Thus we find:

> 'Let none who has a quarrel with his companion join with you until they have been reconciled, that your sacrifice may not be defiled.'[2]

And reconciliation and the kiss of peace duly come together in various authors. We may illustrate the exact use of the Matthew 5.23-24 passage in Cyril of Jerusalem in the fourth century:

> 'Then the deacon cries aloud "Receive one another; and let us kiss one another". Do not think that *this* kiss ranks with those given in public by common friends. it is not of that sort. *This* kiss blends souls with one another, and solicits for them entire forgiveness. Therefore this kiss is the sign that our souls are mingled together, and have banished all remembrance of wrongs. For this cause Christ said 'If you bring your gift [and so on as in Matt. 5] . . . first be reconciled to your brother, and then come and offer your gift." The kiss therefore is reconciliation and for this reason holy: as the blessed Paul has urged in his epistles; "Greet one another with a holy kiss", and Peter ". . . with a kiss of love".'[3]

A similar linking is found (without the actual quotation from Matthew) in the *Apostolic Constitutions* of the same period:

> '[After the departure of the catechumens and the offering of prayers] let that deacon who is at the high priest's hand say to the people, "let no one have any quarrel against another; let no one come in hypocrisy." Then let the men give the men, and the women give the women, the Lord's kiss. But let no one do it with deceit, as Judas betrayed the Lord with a kiss.'[4]

[1] One need hardly multiply texts here, but obvious ones in the Pauline corpus are: Rom. 15.1-2, 5-7; 1 Cor. 11.17-34, 12.21-27, 13. 1-13 (*et passim*); 2 Cor. 13. 13; Gal. 6.1-10; Eph. 4.1-16; Phil.2.1-11; Col. 3.12-17; 1 Thess. 4.3-10; 2 Thess. 1.3-4. The Pastorals are similar—as are Hebrews and the Catholic epistles. Once one starts to look at the epistles from this standpoint, then material about reconciliation and love springs out of almost every page and every chapter. Some of the references above are closely associated with the five references in the Epistles to the kiss.

[2] *Didache* 14 (Jasper and Cuming *op. cit.* p.16).

[3] Cyril of Jerusalem *Mystagogic Catechesis* V.3 (translation in F. L. Cross (ed.) *St. Cyril of Jerusalem's Lectures on the Christian Sacraments* (S.P.C.K., 1951) p.72.).

[4] *Apostolic Constitutions* II, sec. vii (translation from *Ante-Nicene Fathers* Vol. XVIII)—note that the account in *Apostolic Constitutions* VIII differs slightly.

And the quotation from Matthew is found without specific linking with the kiss in both East and West also.[1] The concept of mutual reconciliation is integral to the church's self-understanding in the eucharist in the early centuries, and the kiss is expressive of this and a constant reminder of the need for 'peace'. The social character of the eucharist is a perennial theme.

[1] Obvious early instances are in (in the West) Irenaeus *Adversus Haereses* IV. xviii and (in the East) in the *Didascalia.* Note the teaching based on this verse in the latter:

> 'And the Saviour also said [Matt. 5.23-24]. Now the offering to God is our prayer and eucharist. If then you have some grudge against your brother, or he against you, your prayer will not be heard, and your eucharist will not be accepted . . . by reason of the anger you are harbouring. . . .
>
> 'For this reason, then, O bishops, in order that your offerings and your prayers may be acceptable, when you stand in the church to pray let the deacon say in a loud voice "Is there anyone who holds a grudge against his companion?", so that if there [is] . . . , you can entreat and make peace between them.' (Translation in Sebastian Brock and Michael Vasey (eds.) *The Liturgical Portions of the Didascalia* (Grove Liturgical Study no. 29, 1982) pp.14-15).

One itches to insert a reference to the kiss into passages like this!

3. THE LITURGICAL POSITION OF THE KISS

The evidence cited above suggests that the earliest position for the kiss in both East and West was before the start of the sacramental part of the service. It is not only that the evidence of the authors points to this position—it is also that the rationale concerning reconciliation, and the dependence upon Matthew 5.23-24, naturally point to the same position. This is the position which Dix calls 'classical'[1]. In the Eastern rites the kiss has been relatively stable in this position, but somewhat disturbed by the introduction or movement of other liturgical material.[2]

In the West however we learn from Augustine:

> 'After the Lord's 'Prayer is said "peace be with you": and Christians kiss each other with a holy kiss. The kiss is a sign of peace: just as their lips declare, so let it be morally. That is, as your lips draw near to the lips of your brother, so your heart must not draw away from his heart.'[3]

The Lord's Prayer followed the eucharistic prayer, and the Western rationale tends now to relate the meaning of the kiss to the clause 'Forgive us our sins as we have forgiven those who have sinned against us'. The social aspect is still there, but slightly differently angled.

In 416 we actually catch the change being made. Pope Innocent I writes his famous letter to Decentius, bishop of neighbouring Gubbio, and tells him the Roman position should be followed—as apparently it was not then being. Rome has the same use as Augustine, it seems (and, for all we know, may have had for a hundred years or more), but the other churches in Italy (let alone to the North) still keep the 'classical' position. And thus in time, as the Roman use spread over Western Europe, we find the normal Western position to be after the Lord's Prayer and before communion. In *Ordo Romanus Primus* from around 700 we find it still in congregational use:

> 'When he [the archdeacon] has said, *The peace of the Lord be always with you,* he makes the sign of the cross over the chalice with his hand three times, (and puts a consecrated fragment into it). The archdeacon gives the peace to the chief bishop, then the rest in order and the people likewise.'[4]

The liturgical position is virtually fixed. However the congregational practice is about to change.

[1] G. Dix *The Shape of the Liturgy* (Dacre/Black, 1945) pp.105-110—this is the longest sustained discussion of the kiss I have been able to discover. Dix is ready to say that the theological explanations for another position are adequate enough, but he believes *this* position to be primitive and to have then been universal. One can only concur, though the evidence is obviously somewhat less than conclusive.

[2] In the East the relative positions of the creed (which of course is not found in the earliest rites), the prayers (which are not found as a separate item from the anaphora in the later uses), and the Great Entrance (which has its own separate history) all complicate how the kiss has related to the beginning of the anaphora.

[3] Augustine *Sermo* CCXXVII (translation by COB).

[4] Jasper and Cuming *op. cit.* pp.113-114 (later in the second edition).

4. DECLINE

In both East and West the use of the kiss seems to have fallen away from congregational use during the first millennium. It became a relic only, a formal act between clergy in the sanctuary—usually conducted by a formal touch or greeting of a highly ritualized sort. So it has remained in the Eastern church to this day.[1] The people are greeted with the ancient words. They respond. But they do not kiss. The 'peace' is purely verbal. In the Western church the middle ages saw various residual elements of the kiss still in use. The text remained in the liturgy, as it did in the the East.[2] After the fraction the priest made the sign of the cross thrice over the chalice with a particle of the wafer and led into the standard text:

'Pax Domini sit semper vobiscum' 'Et cum spiritu tuo.'

Then came the commixture, the recitation of Agnus Dei, the prayer for peace[1], and (at high mass) the actual giving of the Pax (for it is by this name it is known) to the assistants—a highly stylized 'kiss'. The congregation were of course not communicant—nor it seems were they pacificant. They were simply not part of the action.

However, there are odd footprints of the original kiss left on the pages of liturgical history, and it is proper to give them a quick look.

Firstly, as the congregational kiss declined, the tendency to kiss everything else but people increased (church doors, statues' feet, altars, stoles, patens, or anything else inanimate). There may of course have been a lay demand behind this—it was not only that the priest was sealed into the sanctuary of the medieval church building, and the congregation was sealed out of it, so that he had only assistants, clothing, and altar to kiss, but also when the clergy were celibate the laity may not have wanted their womenfolk kissed by them. But this is of course the most idle speculation . . .[4]

Secondly, the kissing of the clergy was not confined to the major place in the liturgy indicated above. In the Sarum rite, for instance, the priest kissed the deacon and subdeacon at the foot of the altar steps at the conclusion of the preparatory prayers of penitence. Similarly, the deacon kissed the priest's hand when passing the paten to him during the embolism.

[1] Note the description for instance in John Fenwick *The Eastern Orthodox Liturgy* (Grove Booklet on Ministry and Worship no. 56, 1978) p.20.

[2] The actual word 'peace' is the determinative factor in all the discussion following. Where little or no action is involved, only the word exists to enable us to trace the original intention. In the Eastern liturgies its place has been at the beginning of the anaphora, and in the West after the Lord's Prayer and before communion (see chapter 3 above). This I sometimes call the 'Roman' position.

[3] This prayer, echoing the word 'peace' in the liturgical provision for the 'kiss', is the well-known:

> 'O Lord Jesus Christ, who didst say to thine apostles, "Peace I leave with you, my peace I give unto you"; regard not my sins, but the faith of thy church; vouchsafe to grant unto it that peace and unity which is agreeable to thy will. Who livest and reignest . . .' (ancient translation for an ancient usage).

[4] I naughtily recall my own (very Protestant Irish) lecturer in liturgy, Richard Coates, making passing reference to Roman priests who kiss their stoles because they have no wives. But this would not apply to those who have both stoles and wives.

Thirdly, the laity were not entirely excluded. Instead they were given a substitute.[1] We learn that from the thirteenth century onwards, beginning in England, they received from the sanctuary (via the choir) the 'Pax', which was *not* even a stylized embrace, but was instead 'a tablet with a small picture of Christ which each one kissed'[2] and passed on. This is the meaning of the Sarum rubric *'Let the deacon himself bear the pax unto the rectors of the choir; and let them bring it to the choir . . .'*[3] The tablet was also called 'pax brede' or 'oscularium'.

Fourthly, that initiatory kiss had also been transmuted into something else. It came of course in Hippolytus after the laying on of hands and anointing by the bishop, at the very conclusion of the individual's initiation before he joined in the prayers.[4] Lo and behold, we find in the middle ages (and thus through into the latter part of the twentieth century in the Church of Rome) that this kiss has become a light blow on the cheek at confirmation. The text 'Peace be with you' is in exact linear descent from Hippolytus, but the conventional explanation has apparently been that the newly confirmed is now to take up arms on behalf of Christ.'[5] A case of war *and* peace perhaps?

The Reformation did little to change the picture in the West, A kiss which did not exist was difficult to sustain. It was not directly commanded in scripture, so lacked the imperative which would have led the reformers to restore it. The textual greeting is still sometimes to be found, but its original rationale has now totally disappeared, as the following quotation from Luther shows:

> 'But immediately after the Lord's Prayer shall be said, *The Peace of the Lord,* etc., which is, so to speak, a public absolution of the sins of the communicants, truly the Gospel voice announcing remission of sins . . . On account of this I wish it to be announced with face turned to the people . . .'[6]

Zwingli, Bucer, Calvin and Knox were more thorough and less concerned to conserve traditional material, so the last footprints of the kiss of peace were expunged from their rites. Hermann of Cologne followed a style more akin to Luther's, and retained a verbal greeting.[7] And Cranmer in 1549 did the same.[8]

[1] Thus being present was a substitute for participating. Seeing was a substitute for understanding. Adoring the host was a substitute for receiving. This odd ceremony was a substitute for the kiss. And the use of *pain bénit* was a further substitute for receiving the elements.

[2] G. Podhradsky *New Dictionary of the Liturgy* (1962. English Edition, Chapman, 1966) p.110.

[3] Translation in G. J. Cuming *A History of Anglican Liturgy* (MacMillan, 1969) p.287.

[4] See the text on page 6 above.

[5] See for instance, G. Wainwright *Doxology* (Epworth, 1980) p.484, note 1984.

[6] From Luther's *Formula Missae* of 1523, translation in Jasper and Cuming *op. cit.* p.124 (second edition p.138). Luther is concerned about peace between man and God—justification. The Roman text seemed to offer exactly that. But the *social* purpose of it had entirely disappeared.

[7] *idem* p.146.

[8] Cranmer had Hermann's text in front of him. But in general he was retaining Sarum uses, unless they seemed positively wrong to him. He wrote for the 1549 rite a new liturgical item of his own to follow the peace (printed overleaf):

However, 1552 saw the end of even this liturgical fossil in the Church of England. It was inevitable that it should be moved from its previous place in the rite, as everything between the narrative of institution and the administration had to be removed in order that the latter should follow hard upon the heels of the former. Other material was then relocated in different places in the rite, according to new rationales.[1]

But there was no possible rationale for this redundant greeting between priest and people, and it perished. The Peace was now lost! But Geoffrey Cuming suggests that Cranmer was concerned to conserve the *theme* of God's peace, but had already done so in the new blessing ('The peace of God, with passeth all understanding . . .'—first included in the 1548 *The Order of the Communion*).[2] Thus even the wording was now doubly redundant and doomed to perish, and thus Anglican eucharistic rites remained until the 1960s.[3]

The picture is now complete. In Roman and non-Roman Churches alike, the kiss of peace was missing from worship for hundreds of years, and was apparently never greatly missed. To Christian ears the very notion sounded like an echo of the catacombs, of interest to archaeologists, no doubt, but of no live significance. Even as late as the mid-sixties of this century this remoteness remained.[4] In those days it was not only that no instruction, such as this booklet, existed on the subject—it was rather that no subject existed on which instruction might be given!

Continued from p.13]

> 'Christ our Paschal Lamb is offered up for us, once for all, when he bare our sins in his body on the cross; for he is the very Lamb of God that taketh away the sins of the world; therefore let us keep a joyful and holy feast with the Lord.'

A beautiful bit of work (which, because of its place in the rite, duly perished in 1552—see note 1 below), but one which had nothing to do with the liturgical 'peace'. The latter ran on without anyone knowing what it was for!

[1] For a discussion and explanation of this relocation, see my *What did Cranmer think he was doing?* (Grove Liturgical Study no. 7, 1976 and 1982) pp.21-29.

[2] I do not think this point of Geoffrey Cuming's is in print anywhere at the time of writing, but it is a suggestion he has made to me orally.

[3] A completely different strand of historical investigation would relate to the need and pastoral ministry of reconciliation. The 1549 and 1552 and all succeeding Anglican Prayer Book rites for Holy Communion right down to the twentieth century have begun with rubrics requiring the priest to reconcile to each other members of the congregation who are at enmity, and to restrain them from receiving communion until they are reconciled. Perhaps *theologically* this is the last footprint of the peace left in the Anglican Prayer Books.

[4] I have been amused in writing this booklet to consult the reference works of the 1960s. Thus Gerhard Podhradsky could still write in 1962 (and have reprinted in English as late as 1966):

> 'Today the kiss of peace is given only to the ministers and clergy at a solemn high Mass. Attempts to revive the practice (Pius Parsch) have been tried out in the "token kiss of peace" (practised elsewhere, e.g., Coptic rite) in the form of a handshake between neighbours (thus at the eucharistic Congress in Munich, 1960).' (*op. cit.* p.110)

We would certainly be in an odd case today if the dictionaries were still recording the known instances of the kiss occurring! Similarly J. G. Davies and Raymond George wrote in 1965 about the residual practices among the East Syrians, Maronites, Armenians, and Copts, and then made mention of South India (*A Select Liturgical Lexicon* (Lutterworth, 1965) p.84). But nothing nearer home seems to have been known.

5. RECOVERY

It has all happened astonishingly fast. It certainly began in South India with the rite of the united Church of South Indian in 1950, and this rite consciously and deliberately drew upon Dix' *The Shape of the Liturgy* (though of course it was compiled by Protestant rather than Catholic Christians).[1] The first edition of this rite contained these features:

1. In the 'INTRODUCTION', under the subheading 'THE BREAKING OF THE BREAD', comes this instruction:

   > 'The "Peace" may be given by the presbyter to those with him at the Table, and by them to those in front of the congregation, who will turn in their places and give to those behind them, till all have received it. It is given by a touch of both hands.'[2]

2. In 'THE SERVICE OF THE LORD'S SUPPER', under the subheading 'THE BREAKING OF THE BREAD', the sacramental section begins as follows:

   > *'All stand for the Offertory, and the presbyter shall say:*
   >
   > Behold, how good and joyful a thing it is, brethren, to dwell together in unity.
   >
   > We who are many are one bread, one body, for we all partake of the one bread.
   >
   > I will offer in his dwelling an oblation with great gladness, I will sing and speak praises unto the Lord.
   >
   > *The "Peace" may be given here.*
   >
   > *The bread and wine for the Communion, together with the gifts of the people, are now placed on the Table.'*[3]

allowing the 'peace', but with words which mixed up the concept of unity with that of offering gifts.

In the second and third editions the instruction in the Introduction became bolder.[4] The text however remained virtually unchanged still.

[1] The debt to Dix is obvious in the 'four-action shape' (and probably in the kiss of peace), and is acknowledged by all those concerned. See, for instance, T. S. Garrett *Worship in the Church of South India* (Lutterworth, 1958) p.13.

[2] Synod of CSI *The Service of the Lord's Supper or the Holy Eucharist* (Oxford, 1950) p.vii.

[3] *Idem* p.10.

[4] The text of the second and third editions (the latter to be found in the CSI *Book of Common Worship* (Oxford, 1963) p.xiii) is as follows (a variant in the second edition is shown in square brackets):

> 'When the Peace is given, the giver places his right palm against the right palm of the receiver, and each closes his left hand over the other's right hand. The Peace is given before the offertory (see Matthew 5.23, 24) as a sign of fellowship, and the offertory sentences recall St. Augustine's teaching that the sacrifice we offer is our unity in Christ. The presbyter gives the Peace to those ministering with him, and these in turn give it to the congregation. It may be passed through the congregation either along the rows, or from those in front to those behind. [It is suggested that] Each person as he gives the Peace may say in a low voice "The peace of God", or "The peace of God be with you".'

To this day, these latter texts to be said by one person to another rank as almost the only official guidance to be found anywhere in the texts. (But see page 24, footnote 4, below).

The compilers of the CSI Liturgy claim at this point to be dependent not solely on Dix, but also upon the continuing use of the peace in the Indian Christians of St. Thomas, who derive from the Syrians.[1] It is doubtful whether the actual touching of hands passed instantaneously and joyfully into widespread use in South India, for congregations retained their traditional liturgies usually—as, e.g. amongst ex-Anglicans the 1662 BCP—and the introduction of the united liturgy was slow and hesitant. But a blow had been struck, and it remained struck.

That was 1950. Progress into the parent Churches of South India (in the West) was slow. We have seen already how unknown the kiss was in Europe in the mid-sixties. The reports of the Liturgical Commissions of Anglicans in England and America in the 1950s had not mentioned it.[2] The new Anglican rites in Hong Kong (1957), Canada (1959)' Japan (1959), West Indies (1959), and India, Pakistan, Burma, and Ceylon (1960) have no mention of touching each other, though all but the Hong Kong rite have a versicle and response more or less in the Roman position—presumably influenced by the sheer magic of Rome rather by any actual rationale of this particular fossil.[3] The Lambeth Conference of 1958, which devoted a whole section to the revision of the Book of Common Prayer, and made some notable advances (as well as some movements in other directions) in thinking about eucharistic liturgy, was also silent about the peace.[4] The time was not yet. The restoration in Anglican rites came in due course by two main routes:

1. Although South India had not directly affected the 1958 Lambeth Conference, it did affect the next Anglican eucharistic rite to be written, namely *A Liturgy for Africa* in 1964. Leslie Brown was the draftsman for this rite, and now affected a clear division between 'THE PEACE' (a clear cross-heading) and 'THE PLACING OF THE GIFTS'—in that order. The rubric which followed the versicle and response reads as follows:

   > *'Or the Priest may touch hands with those in the Sanctuary, saying the same words, and they in turn may pass the greeting in like manner to the people.'*

   This liturgy, not used much itself, has in turn influenced other Anglican usage elsewhere.[5]

2. The Church of England included in Series 2 communion in 1967 the provision shown overleaf (which came just before 'THE PREPARATION OF THE BREAD AND WINE').

[1] L. W. Brown *Relevant Liturgy* (S.P.C.K., 1965) p.60.

[2] The reports in view here are the American *Prayer Book Studies IV* (Church Pension Fund, 1953) and the English Liturgical Commission's *Prayer Book Revision in the Church of England* (S.P.C.K., 1957).

[3] All these rites are contained in B. J. Wigan (ed.) *The Liturgy in English* (Oxford, 1962 and 1964), except the Hong Kong rite which is in my *Modern Anglican Liturgies 1958-1968* (Oxford, 1968).

[4] See *The Lambeth Conference 1958* (Seabury/S.P.C.K., 1958) 2.78-94.

[5] The text of *A Liturgy for Africa* is in Brown *op. cit.* and in my *Modern Anglican Liturgies 1958-1968.* In the latter work I trace out the general impact of that liturgy on other Anglican texts.

'22. *Then the Priest may say,*
We are the body of Christ. By one Spirit we were all baptized into one body. Endeavour to keep the unity of the Spirit in the bond of peace.
The peace of the Lord be always with you;
And with thy spirit.'

This text had its limitations—particularly in that it came straight after the penitential section in a rite which included no guidance on posture, and thus tended to be said with the congregation kneeling, and without any actual sight of each other—let alone contact. It was also optional, but (perhaps because of the Anglican tendency to read stuff as part of the service if it is there in print under the clergyman's nose) it passed into common usage. The new Pauline text started to become part of people's liturgical landscape.

Series 3, authorized from 1973, took this much further. Now there was some coaching in opening Note 11:

'THE PEACE (22). The president may accompany the words of the Peace with a handclasp or similar action: and both the words and action may be passed through the congregation.'

The text itself ran as follows:

'THE PEACE

21 *Stand*
President We are the body of Christ. In the one Spirit we were all baptized into one body. Let us then pursue all that makes for peace and builds up our common life.

22 *The President gives the Peace to the congregation saying:*
The peace of the Lord be always with you.
All **And also with you.**'

This ensured its position in the rite, ensured it was taken standing, and strongly hinted that it might best be an action and not only words. It is likely that it was the introduction of Series 3—the 'green booklet'—which led at the same time to the introduction of an actual *action* of greeting at the Peace in many congregations in England. And Series 3 has had considerable impact in other parts of the world.

Other Anglicans were slightly slower starting. 'The Pan-Anglican Document' on 'The Structure and Contents of the Eucharistic Liturgy' in 1965 had no mention of the Peace.[1] The American *Prayer Book Studies XVII* in 1967 was equally silent, and it was only in the 'Green Book' in 1970 that any textual provision was made by American Episcopalians.[2]

[1] The text of this is in *Modern Anglican Liturgies 1958-1968.*

[2] The text of the 'Green Book' (1970) and 'Zebra Book' (1973) rites is in my next volume *Further Anglican Liturgies 1968-1975* (Grove Books, 1975). The final development in America is in the new *Book of Common Prayer* (1977 and 1979), and the texts in that book have not yet been collected into my yet-to-come volume.

New Zealand, Australia, and South Africa, seem to have picked up the practice in the second half of the 1960s from *A Liturgy from Africa* or from the Church of England. The second 'Pan-Anglican Document' was published in 1969 (again with Leslie Brown as a drafter). and this time the Peace was mentioned briefly, though in an odd way.[1] In the 1970s, perhaps in line with the actual Series 3 usage in England, the practice has spread into virtually all the new rites.

Roman Catholics have progressed in a similar way. The Peace is not actually mentioned in the Vatican II *Constitution on the Sacred Liturgy* (1963). The first 'Instruction' on putting the Constitution into effect plays down the kissing of objects, without playing up the kissing of people. But that is only in 1964. By the time that the 'General Instruction' accompanied the new order of the mass (*Missa Normativa*) in 1970, there was plenty of reference to the Peace. The General Instruction says 'Before they share in the same bread, the people express their love for one another . . .'[2] And the text of the mass adds to the versicle and response 'Let us offer each other the sign of peace', and goes on to say that the greeting follows local custom.

This progress in the texts, from an action unknown in the early sixties to that which is confidently assumed to be happening everywhere in the seventies, relates closely to liturgical renewal in all sorts of other ways. The growing emphasis upon the church as the body of Christ, and the corresponding importance of the horizontal relationships involved, have spilled into virtually all the areas of the liturgy, and the kiss of peace is only one expression, albeit a key one, of these new emphases. It is certainly *not,* as it would have been to Dix, a disinterring of a long-buried notion, solely on the grounds that it was primitive or even 'classical'. Rather, the proposals of the liturgists have chimed in with the growing self-consciousness of the church as the people of God. This might even be related in Western Europe and North America to the passing of Christendom and the reversion to pre-Constantinian understandings of the role of the church in the world. And the revival of the peace has marched alongside the growth of charismatic renewal, fuelling it and being fuelled by it. And in *that* context, whatever coynesses the texts express, we really are talking about a kiss . . .

[1] The Peace is grouped with 'The Prayers', apparently as the conclusion of the ante-communion. (See *Further Anglican Liturgies 1968-1975* pp.17, 27, 29). Although this is a conceivable interpretation of Justin and Hippolytus, and it certainly ensures that the Peace does not drift into the Roman position, yet it is at odds with the presentation of all the texts, which invariably group the Peace with the sacramental liturgy.

[2] *General Instruction* para 56(b) (to be found, for instance, in *Instructions on the Revised Roman Rites* (Collins Liturgical Publications, 1979) p.96).

6. THE ALTERNATIVE SERVICE BOOK 1980

In Rite A no initial coaching about the Peace is now included in the opening Notes, though, oddly enough, the words found in the 'Green Booklet' *are* reprinted at the beginning of Rite B.[1] In both rites permission is given in the Notes to have the Peace at other points in the rite than the one at which it is printed.

In rite A the textual changes as follows:

1. Two texts are printed in the main service for the president to use, and a rubric allows the use of *'other suitable words'* with a cross-reference to section 83 in the appendices, where a selection of seasonal suggestions is offered. It is clear that the president may well write his own introductory texts for this section in place of any of those offered.

2. The new text in the main provision is the first one 'Christ is our peace . . .'. this was added by the Revision Committee in 1979 because the previous text ('We are the body of Christ . . .') was thought to end with a slightly wearying hortatory note. The new one was drawn partly from the Scottish Episcopal Church's 'Orange Bookie' of 1977,[2] partly from Ephesians 2.

3. After the versicle and response a new section has been added:

   'The president may say

   Let us offer one another a sign of peace.

   and all may exchange a sign of peace.'

   This section is an unashamed borrowing from Rome.[3] It has had the odd effect of making congregations which previously swung straight into the Peace after the presidents greeting of them now hesitate and wait for some further triggering by him.

Rite B in the main text, just as in the opening Notes, represents roughly where developments had reached in 1976, the year its immediate ancestor (Series 1 and 2 Revised) was authorized. There is only one presidential lead-in ('We are the body of Christ . . .'), no provision for appendixed or home-made substitutes, and no mention of 'Let us offer one another . . .'. Rite B lovers may well complain that the ASB does not take them as seriously as it does Rite A lovers[4], but as it is unlikely that they will be wishing to experiment with the Peace, whilst being conservative on language, there is probably little reason for them to complain.

[1] See p.17 above.

[2] The Scottish text reads:

'Priest: We meet in Christ's name: let us share his peace.

All: Peace be with you.'

[3] See p.18 opposite.

[4] But then the ASB was meant to be a collection of modern-language services. Rite B got in half by accident, and without any principles agreed in advance for true adaptation of it to conform in its provisions to Rite A.

7. WHERE? WHY? HOW?

We come now to the coaching part of this booklet. It is inevitably subjective. And, judging by the recent pace of change, it may soon be out of date.[1] But, for what it is worth in Easter week 1982 as I write it, here it is.

Where?

Where in the rite should the Peace come? The provision for it to occur elsewhere in Rite A, away from its official 'hinge' position at the beginning of 'The ministry of the Sacrament', actually arose from two causes, which happily coincided. Roughly, these causes may be categorized as 'catholic' and 'evangelical', and the reasoning needs some inspection.

It has already emerged above at what point in the rite the 'catholic' alternative position comes. Where there is a desire to follow Rome, which occasionally means that a congregation was actually using the Missa Normativa in the 1970s but has now decided to use Rite A (with a very careful choice of options and some embellishment in all likelihood), then the Roman position for the Peace, virtually last thing before communion, has its attractions. In favour of it also may be urged amongst Anglicans that the texts which accompany the breaking of the bread often relate to the unity of the body of Christ (drawing upon 1 Corinthians 10.16-17), and that there is thus a grouping of ideas at one point in the rite—for the 'social' character of the Lord's Prayer leads naturally into both the breaking and the Peace.[2] The American Book of Common Prayer allows this position also.[3]

The 'evangelical' alternative arises not from the knowledge of events elsewhere, but rather from ignorance about liturgy, combined with a robust commonsense about what we do in church. Why do I have to wait half the service before I am allowed to greet the brother sitting next to me? So goes the question—and, as there is often no great knowledge of antiquity and its reasoning, the tendency then is to have a mutual greeting at the beginning. This can effect introductions, enable people to relax about their otherwise silent (and perhaps even tight-lipped) neighbours in church, and generally join the congregation together. It remains a far more open question as to whether this is the *eucharistic* Peace—and of course evangelicals are fully ready to employ it for non-sacramental services as well as sacramental ones.[4]

I doubt whether either of the above variants should be preferred to the position printed in the ASB and in general use among Anglicans

[1] See the Preface on page 2 about speed of change.

[2] Thus Crichton writes about the Roman position 'The sign of peace and the fraction are closely associated.' *(Christian Celebration: The Mass* (Geoffrey Chapman, 1971) p.97). But although they are juxtaposed in the Roman rite the words which accompany the fraction do not have this love and unity theme at all—unlike the Anglican references to 1 Cor. 10.16-17.

[3] Permission is given to use the Roman position in the American *Book of Common Prayer* on p.407.

[4] And apparently they could even cite Tertullian as well as Paul as possible precedents (see quotation on p.7 above)!

thoughout the world.[1] Whilst the position at the beginning of the service does not take the congregation far enough into the eucharist, the Roman position takes them too far. If we hold onto the rationale that reconciliation and mutual recognition in Christ are of the essence of the Peace, then the congregation ought not to begin upon the eucharist before establishing 'peace'. It is the exchange of peace which *qualifies* the congregation to celebrate the eucharist.

On the other hand, whatever need there may be for introductions at the beginning of a service (or simply greetings between friends), congregations would do better to work at informal ways of ensuring that members welcome each other at that point, without anticipating the eucharistic 'Peace'.[2]

The given position is particularly appropriate when other special events occur within the eucharistic context. These are almost the test cases, exposing the other two positions as too late or too early in the rite. When a baptism, confirmation, marriage, ordination, restoration of lapsed (e.g. by renewal of baptismal vows), or ministry of healing is placed after the ministry of the word and before the ministry of the sacrament, then the greeting is the wholly appropriate next event in the rite, and other positions would be absurd. Justin and Hippolytus come into their own on just these occasions.

This is not to say that there are *never* occasions for a 'once-off' variant. There have been farewell occasions in St. John's Chapel where we have *ended* the rite with the kiss. And when a congregation is sitting down together to an agape (including eucharist) then the kiss *might* more meaningfully come at the beginning.

Why?

What then is the rationale of the kiss? If we gather together the ancient and modern precedents and theologizing, we come up with certain themes which cluster round the event. It is unlikely that congregations which practice the Peace will know *why* they do so—and even more unlikely that those which refrain from any action understand any positive rationale. The restoration of the practice has—amazingly, it would seem—outmarched any teaching or instruction about it. Where it has gone well, it is as though it had touched some deep instinct positively—and where it has not gone well, the reverse is probably true. Such instincts should not be despised, but there *must* be things to be said for minds to grasp, surely? Here then is the 'cluster' of themes.

[1] Simple expressions of welcome, even of love, as people meet for worship are very appropriate both as between good friends, and when making guests or newcomers welcome. Without distorting existing (sacrosanct!) seating plans based upon fixed pews, a long loving forward move can be achieved if worshippers learn *to go along pews on entry,* so as to leave space for later comers to feel welcomed, whereupon a smile underlines the point. When worshippers guard the ends of pews, and cling to the aisle seats, then later comers feel unwelcome, have to push their way in if they go near such pews at all, and cannot be greeted in a relaxed way by the embattled end-seat-holders who are grudgingly pulling in their stomachs or twisting their hips to let in the later arrivals! A simple lesson about love can be learned here, but Anglicans are a long way generally from having learned it.

1. **Recognition**. Others are in Christ with us, and at the Peace we give them full recognition. The church in other words re-establishes its identity by this mutuality—each also recognizing Christ in the other. Such recognition is based on the objective standing in Christ of others, and that is the starting-point for the further rationales which are to follow here. The affirmation here is independent of considerations of liking or disliking others—it is a 'holy' kiss, recognizing the 'holy' people. This may of course leave a question open as to whether non-communicants who are present can or should be so greeted, and it is acknowledged that the readiness to have them present raises a theoretical problem. Hippolytus and other early authors would have thought it scandalous to have even catechumens present for the Peace—how then can we do it?

   The easiest response is to say that Hippolytus would have been equally opposed to letting non-communicants join in the prayers, and these have long since been open to outsiders, in a way that the distribution of communion itself is not. It is a pity if in places the Peace includes outsiders (and thus ceases to mark out the insiders), but it may well be better than excluding them at this point. This is doubly forceful in that the children of believers *must* be included, even if in England they are still ex-communicated until they are confirmed. The peace is a further witness that they are 'in Christ' with us.

2. **Reconciliation.** This theme has run throughout the historical treatment. Actual known offences of one against another may be rare, but hostility and lack of acceptance is often found today. The call of Christ to his people is to go to the other side of the building if necessary to get at peace with another brother, rather than simply hug those whom you would be ready to hug from natural affection anyway. It should be impossible to share the Peace and remain at odds with each other. There is need for a little time and space for movement . . . And the sheer existence of the Peace ought to prompt believers to be at peace *before* they come.

3. **Welcome.** Strangers should be welcomed in Christ at this point, and made 'at home' in this congregation.[1]

4. **Affirmation and love.** Unafraid bodily contact establishes a bond. It should be reinforced by 'eye-contact' and words unembarrassedly spoken to each other.

5. **Joy.** The hint of this which was discussed on page 8 above seems to be an authentic Christian note. Being in Christ, being a fellowship, loving each other, being in touch literally with each other, approaching the feast of love—these all produce a bloom

[1] I once preached at a eucharist in New Zealand, and at the Peace was introduced (in Christ) to relatives of mine whom I had never met before, was not expecting to encounter in worship, and had not previously known were 'in Christ'. So there was both recognition and welcome . . .

of joy upon the relationships. It is much to be prized in Christian worship. And our joy in Christ cannot be taken away even by saddening events (John 16.20-24, Phil. 4.4, etc.)

6. **General effect.** If the themes above are running through the Peace, then the overall effect ought to help the church be the church, as a community of worship, fellowship, wholeness, and mission. The leaders of worship ought constantly to have an eye to these great aims of serving God, serving him, that is, through the building up of the church, and should not be content simply to get the Peace to 'go well'.

There are ramifications of such themes (the role of a loving community in national and local politics, for instance?), and congregations ought to work at them. The problem is not that churches are running off too fast into the ramifications, but that they have not yet well established the central ground.

How?

Despite the title of this booklet, by the time the present period is being considered the event is being called the 'Peace' rather than the 'Kiss of Peace'! It is clear that kissing in the Old and New Testaments implied at the very least an embrace, almost certainly the touching of cheeks, and quite probably the touching of lips. In the early church it remained the same—though it is noticeable that the sexes were usually separated.[1] The quotation from Augustine on page 11 above actually mentions 'lips'. And by these standards the modern revival is thus far (except amongst some charismatics) a fairly weak substitute.

There are two ways of looking at this contrast. It is perfectly possible, for instance, to argue that these affairs are historically (and sometimes geographically or ethnically) conditioned. Thus in the 1940s J. B. Phillips 'translated' the Pauline kiss in his *Letters to Young Churches* as 'I should like you to shake hands all round as a sign of Christian love' (1 Cor. 16.22)! If we persisted with such principles in translating scripture practically everything that was actually Jewish or even ancient would disappear from the Bible, but from a *homiletical* point of view Phillips (it could be argued) cuts a corner usefully. Certainly Dix took a similar line. In his famous description of the grocer from Brondesbury, whom he imagines in the ante-Nicene church undergoing persecution, but still culturally in twentieth century London, he writes:

> 'Then each man turns and grasps his neighbour strongly and warmly by both hands. (I am trying to represent the ancient by a modern convention. The kiss was anciently a much commoner salutation than it is with us in England, but it implied more affection than does merely "shaking hands" with us.)'[2]

On this basis, a double handshake would be the limit today.

The other view would be that embracing and kissing within families still goes on, that such kissing is not under suspicion of eroticism or

[1] See page 9 above. Also the Didascalia chapter 12 (in *The Liturgical Portions of the Didascalia* page 16).

[2] Dix *The Shape of the Liturgy* p.142.

other Hollywood influences, that the Christian church should be viewing itself as a family, and that a warm embrace is entirely appropriate—not only restoring the biblical kiss, but also witnessing that kissing has richer and wider meanings than solely eroticism.

Perhaps the conditioning factor requires that we are also sensitive to other background factors in today's world. It is interesting that in the Korean liturgy of 1973 the rubric reads *'Each person bows to those standing near him'*[1]—a practice reflecting the oriental provenance of the rite. Thus it might be that the general aim should be to have a practice which is warm and affectionate, related to local secular custom but ready to challenge it mildly without outraging opinion unnecessarily, and open to further development. Whilst it is easier to call it the 'Peace' it may be more prophetic to call it the 'kiss' . . .

What is certain is that we are now well beyond the point where the greeting was passed through the congregation as though it were an alms-dish or a relay baton.[2] The general developing pattern has in recent years been for all to turn at once and greet their neighbours, and for the more extrovert or determined to move in search of others to greet also. Where the clergy or other ministers are separated from the congregation by any distance, it is usual for them to bridge this gap at the beginning of the greeting, but choirs and organists also have claims upon their affection.

In fact, the kiss needs plenty of space. It is insufficient from the point of view of its rationale for worshippers to be too closely boxed in with others and imprisoned in long straight pews. Whilst many other considerations of space and furnishings have to be considered, yet in essence the kiss of peace needs room for people to move about, to seek each other out a bit, and to express themselves as outgoing. This has been evident in the discussion above under 'Why?' It is helped where worshippers do not sit in straight rows, but can see each other's faces.

Another feature of the 'How?' is the question of what to say to each other. The initial formal pattern is to say 'The Peace of the Lord be with you' in imitation of the president's greeting of the congregation. But minds soon move on beyond that, and the informal address to each other is often conditioned by existing relationships, known needs, and the particular occasion. Names are freely used. Just as with actions, so with words—the approach to another, perhaps shyer, member of the community must be sensitive to what he or she is ready to accept as well as expressing what the approacher is wanting to give! Despite the South Indian[3] (and Australian[4]) suggestions of words, it is likely that specifically printed words will now no more serve each occasion than will detailed instructions about the action. The kiss has acquired its own momentum. There is good hope that this is of God.

[1] *Further Anglican Liturgies 1968-1975* p.307.

[2] See the Liturgical Commission's *Commentary* on the ASB, p.76, note 32, where this is dismissed as the 'Daisy-chain' or 'Domino' theory!

[3] See footnote 4 on page 15 above.

[4] In *An Australian Prayer Book* (1978) there comes the suggestion: 'When circumstances permit [sic!], all may exchange the greeting, saying, for example, "Peace be with you" . . .' (*op. cit.* p.154).